As if it were Yesterday

URSULA WILDE

Autobiography

Dedication

I want to dedicate this book to my sons Clifford and Jon, their wives Sandra and Gillian and my wonderful grandchildren Lucy, Callam, Nathan and Sadie, my brother Bobby's children, Wayne, Tracy, Tina, Emma, Jason and Lee and their mum Brenda.

First Published by Ursula Wilde

Copyright © 2014 Ursula Wilde

The right of Ursula Wilde to be identified as the author of this work has been asserted by him in accordance with the Copyright, Design and Patents Act 1988.

British Library Cataloguing in Publication Data.
A catalogue record for this book is available from the British Library.

ISBN 9780993261008

Printed and bound in the UK by
Custom Print, 13-23 Naylor Street, Liverpool, Merseyside L3 6DR
www.customprintgroup.co.uk

CONTENTS

Foreword

When I met (Shena) Ursula it was at a
charity night at Peel Hall, Liverpool.
She was so glad we asked her to join
our Jazz Band, this was in the late 50s - 60s.

We played many a venue with
Richard Stilgoe on piano including
Caldy 7s Rugby Club, Iron Door, Storyville,
Oddspot - Bold Street and many others.

It was a great time in my life and was the
start of the Mersey Beat - I still play today.

Brian Hall
Guitarist & Songwriter

Brian just in the picture on the left playing guitar,
Dave Dickson on the right on saxaphone and now runs
'Perninsula Jazz Band', Leo in the middle on clarenet.
Brian wrote the hit song 'Amanda' sung by
Stuart Gillies in the 70's.

Introduction

My parents, Robert and Ursula Hulse (née Roberts) came from families with fascinating histories so I shall begin my memoir by telling you about them...

Chapter One

Part One – The Roberts Family

This strand of my story begins long, long ago when my great great grandfather, Thomas Roberts, born in about 1831 in Thornton Hough, married a Brimstage girl named Elizabeth, and they made their home in Bromborough. Their children were Robert, Elizabeth and Emma. Thomas was a coachman and, in those far-off days when wealthy people lived in the local large houses, there were good opportunities for coachmen and family accommodation was provided.

At first, Thomas worked for Mr Robert Rankin, a merchant with a business in Liverpool, who had taken a lease on Bromborough Hall in 1851. The Hall was a very grand house with beautiful grounds stretching right down to the River Mersey, where Matalan stands now; there were several service cottages and Thomas and Elizabeth lived in what had been an old lodge to the Hall, but by then renamed Rose Cottage, close to where Tebay Road is now situated.

In time, Robert, my great grandfather, followed in Thomas's footsteps and became a coachman too. He married Elizabeth, a Trefnant girl, who was always known as Rosina. By 1881 baby David had been born, soon to be followed by Robert Alfred (Alf) and they lived in a tiny cottage in The Weint, off Allport Lane; the little building is still there, set back along the narrow entry between the old Nat West Bank and the health food premises. It is hard to imagine how they fitted in. Three more children were born, John (Jack), Elizabeth (Mally) and then Eliza. However, during those years, the family moved to Robert's old home, Rose Cottage, which offered much more accommodation; in 1891, they even had two lodgers. Since 1873, Mr Robert Norris Dale and family had been living at Bromborough Hall, after the Rankins had moved away. Mr Dale was a much respected insurance underwriter with the British and Foreign Marine Insurance in Liverpool. The whole family soon became much involved in the life of Bromborough, supporting the Parish Church and the community in general, much as the Rankins had done.

Bromborough Hall stood on the site where Matalan is today. Grandmother Emma Lydia Roberts worked here as cook for Sir William Forwood for many years in the 1920s and 30s.

From 1893 to 1898, Colonel Rigby was at the Hall, and Robert and his family continued to live at Rose Cottage where Edward was born in 1895. Alfred, always one to look to the future, went to sea at the age of 15, signing on as a crew member on a voyage to the United States of America. He was greatly impressed by the experience, witnessing at first hand the beginnings of the motor car industry; this could well have been the inspiration for his later ventures. His wages were a welcome 'nest egg' and he was fortunate in being one of only 10 of the crew to have been unaffected by the outbreak of yellow fever on the return voyage.

Another family move was prompted by the death of my great grandfather Robert in about 1900. Rosina, now a widow, with her six children, was offered a small service cottage in White Row, very close to Bromborough Hall, and next to the Hall Farm. In the 1901 census, David was listed as a carpenter, Alf was a groom and Jack did general work; Mally, Eliza and Edward would have attended the village school. 'Ellin', Rosina's sister, was a visitor; now, how did they all fit in that tiny cottage?

Bromborough Village School
My mother Ursula and her Brothers went to this school.
Mr J P King was the headmaster from 1897 - 1939.

By now, the next resident had arrived at Bromborough Hall, having moved there in 1898; he was Sir William Bower Forwood, a notable gentleman who had shipping and other commercial interests in Liverpool where he had been Mayor in 1880. Sir William was to be of particular assistance to Alf in years to come.

By 1906, Alf was ready to start his own business, beginning in a small way by opening a cycle repair place in The Weint where it remained the base for his enterprise for a few years. However, another, even more significant event in Alf's life, occurred in 1907 when he married Emma Lydia Rowell, who was originally from Huntingdonshire, but who had been working at Benham, a large house in Spital Road, Bromborough, and later at the Hall itself, where her newly acquired cookery skills became well known and much appreciated. Alf and Emma were able to purchase No. 58 The Rake where their daughter, Ursula, my mother, was born in 1909; Ursula's two brothers, my uncles Claude and Ken were soon to follow. Next door at No. 56 lived my great aunt 'Mally' and her husband Tommy Clapperton. Later on, they were to become founder members of the Bromborough Branch of the Royal British Legion.

Well, what about Rosina? I had been told years ago, that she had been a midwife; sure enough, the local directory for 1902 records that very profession for her. Eventually, Rosina moved to No. 7 The Rake, still actively involved in her skilled work, long before the NHS was established of course.

I was very interested to learn that my grandad Alf was recorded in the 1911 census as a Candle Packer showing that he was employed at Price's Patent Candle Company at Bromborough Pool, while he was gradually building up a clientele for his bicycle repair business in The Weint.

Meanwhile, Emma's baking skills continued to be noteworthy. I remember my mother telling me of Lady Forwood's visits to my grandparents' home; they were important occasions and Nan taught my mother how to curtsy. Often enough Lady Forwood came to their house after Church on a Sunday; in summer, to complement her elegant dress, a parasol was carried. The usual greeting was followed by, 'I've come for a cup of tea and a piece of your wonderful currant cake', a well-remembered expression!

My mother, Ursula, and her brothers, Claude and Ken, all attended the village school. As soon as she was old enough, Ursula went straight from the classroom, at the end of the school day, to her father's bicycle repair premises to 'braid' the rear wheels of the ladies' bicycles, to prevent their skirts from catching in the wheels. At the village school, the Headmaster was Mr J.P. (Jimmy) King, well-remembered, even today; he retired in 1939, having been appointed in 1897. My mother always praised his teaching and believed that it contributed to her own success. Later, she attended the Arnham Ladies' College in Hamilton Square, and gained her qualification in Accountancy; this was to be of invaluable assistance to her when she was, for many years, running the garage office.

By 1919, Alf was ready for his next business venture, as a Motor and Cycle Repairer. The aptly named Roberts Garage with its one petrol pump, was located in premises at the end of a former barn facing Bromborough Cross. Between Alf's enterprise and the Church Institute, the path led up to Bromborough Smithy; Gerald (popularly known as Gerry or Gag) Sheridan, the blacksmith and his brother Leo, had followed in their father Lawrence's occupation, Leo at Lower Bebington and Gerry in Bromborough where he is so well-remembered, shoeing horses and fettling ironwork, to the fascination of old and young alike. Both brothers had served as farriers to the Denbighshire Yeomanry in the First World War, a reminder of the extent to which horses were used during that conflict. How interesting it is to realise that, side by side, the smithy and the motor and bicycle businesses flourished, and knowing that, gradually, the motor transport would, in large part, replace horses and horse drawn vehicles as a normal method of transport.

Sheridans Smithy was situated between the Church Hall opposite
Bromborough Cross, the little opening next to Barclays Bank,
the house was next to the Smithy. 'Gag' Sheridan is seen on the right.

Grandad Alf, very farsightedly, commenced his own taxi service at The Cross and he was soon ready for his next venture, a purpose built garage in a new location. At that time, in the 1920's, there was no Bromborough by-pass, all traffic used the road right through the village, and it was becoming quite a problem, so much so that Sir William Forwood and others living locally , requested the local council to set a speed limit, so on 24 April 1924, a limit was duly set at 12 mph! Even so, the density of traffic continued to grow and, in due course, the need for a by-pass came under discussion.

Grandad saw his opportunity; I was told that Sir William had suggested that a site close to the junction with Allport Road, would fulfil Alf's aspirations. How fortunate it was that a friend of Sir William, a Mr Woodfin, a cotton broker, very obligingly came up with a loan of £1,000, a very large sum of money in those days, the average wage being about £2 per week. Naturally, the Roberts family felt quite overwhelmed! However, some people thought that the site was too far from the village to be a success.

Of course, planning permission had to be sought. The Bebington Urban District Council minutes provide invaluable details, including a follow-up request which was approved on 19 December 1925 - 'Application received from Mr R.A. Roberts was submitted with regard to storage of petrol, 1,000 gallons in petrol pump in connection with his newly-erected premises at corner of Allport Road and New Chester Road.' The Application was approved.

A cottage-style house was built alongside the garage. The petrol tanks had to be dug out, so Uncle Claude and my mother rolled up their sleeves and helped to excavate the large hole needed. Mother told me that it had been very hard work, but they were an ambitious family and were looking to the future. Roberts Garage was credited with being the first one to be built on this part of the A41 and, contrary to some local opinion, it proved to be a great success.

Mother had already learnt to drive when in her early teens; there were no tests in those days, so when she had gained her accountancy qualification, she was well equipped to work in the new premises' office. One day, a young man named Robert Hulse, driving a lovely red MG car, stopped for petrol; he was dashing and handsome and swept her off her feet! They courted for ten years, at first going to dances held at the Eastham Ferry Ballroom, behind the hotel. Of course, the woods, the lovely gardens and the numerous other attractions were still very popular, even though the days of Blondin, the tightrope performer and of Houdini, the escapologist, were just distant memories, even for the older people.

Mother and her two brothers formed a talented musical trio; Claude played the fiddle, Ken was on the drums and Mother was the pianist. As well as their daily work in the garage, in their spare time they played for local parties at, for example, the local Council Offices in Allport Lane, just next to where the Civic Centre now stands. Other venues were some of the larger houses in the district, one was Ashfield, the Taveners' residence in Allport Road, where the Westminster Drive estate now stands. Another example was Plymyard House where the Ravenscrofts lived in the 1920s and 30s; Mr Leslie Ravenscroft was a cotton broker in Liverpool. The family later moved to Burton where their son John was born. He joined his father's firm, but then decided to change his surname; as John Peel, he became a very famous disc jockey, a 'far cry' from a career in the cotton trade!

My parents were married in 1936 at St Barnabas Parish Church in Bromborough, and I duly arrived the next year, but now I should like to relate the story of my father's family and what an interesting tale it is.

My parents wedding – Ursula Roberts and Robert Hulse in 1936 at St Barnabas Church in Bromborough Village.

Part Two – The Hulse Family

In Victorian times, Liverpool was growing rapidly. George Hulse senior, my great great grandfather, born in Chester in about 1813, was attracted by Liverpool's many opportunities for entrepreneurs. Around 1840 he set up in business there in Dale Street as a Dealer in Birds. A skilled naturalist, he soon broadened his horizons by importing various species of exotic animals, for example lions which were then housed in separate blocks of properties in Dale Street. The animals were then sold to circuses and zoos. One of his clients was William Manders whose Menagerie and Foreign Legion of Birds and Beasts was a very popular attraction, travelling to major cities and towns, especially in the 1860s. Among his other clients were Sir Robert Sanger's famous Circus, and Dublin Zoo.

I am told that George even had a small fleet of ships to convey the animals from abroad. Trade with the West Indies provided turtles, a popular delicacy, especially for the well-to-do. The turtles were not only sold live to such places as the Adelphi Hotel where, I am told, the turtle-tanks are still to be seen in the basement, but also the fresh meat could be purchased at George's shop in Dale Street where the turtle tanks were placed strategically in the window to attract customers. Not content with that and with a ready supply of turtles, a soup-processing factory was established in Vauxhall. The finished product found a ready sale, being supplied, so I was told, to no less a personage than Queen Victoria herself – though I have yet to discover if a Royal Warrant had been issued!

Another noteworthy event was the donation of an extremely large turtle shell to the newly built Liverpool Museum which was opened in 1860 in William Brown Street. The gift was particularly appropriate since, in 1851, Lord Derby's extensive zoological collection had been donated to Liverpool's temporary museum in Duke Street, before it was transferred to the grand purpose-built one in William Brown Street. The new museum proved to be a permanent and fitting location for the collection's ever-growing popularity.

George (senior) and his wife, Ann, had six children, of whom George (junior), my great grandfather, was the eldest, born in 1844.

Just about everyone will have seen a real lion, either in a zoo or on a wildlife reserve, or at least one shown on television, but how about being with one at very close quarters? Here is my family's story: George (senior) was well-used to lions and their behaviour, so it was only natural that young George absorbed that knowledge. He became a skilled and competent handler to the extent that he was able to enter the cage, confident that he would be safe. However, in February 1864, he was at Dublin Zoo, inspecting four lions which the Hulses had supplied to the Zoological Gardens. A small group of friends had been invited to witness George's skill, but what George did not know was that, before his arrival, a lively terrier, brought by one of the group, had disturbed the lions. George entered the enclosure, only to be savagely attacked; badly mauled, he was rushed off to hospital where skilled surgery, including 68 stitches, repaired much of the damage. Evidently young George had a very strong constitution as he lived to the ripe old age of 83, albeit with a damaged arm.

Do you believe in coincidences? well, here is one: in 2012, I happened to be in Dublin with a friend, researching the Wilde family tree; unfortunately I fractured my wrist, so off we went to the Cottage Hospital. While waiting for the plaster to be applied, I happened to notice a plaque on the wall; it stated that Mr George Hulse had been the first patient to have had microsurgery performed successfully – I could hardly believe my eyes!

Now, back to Liverpool. George Hulse (senior) continued to run the turtle business, with young George assisting and gradually taking over more of the responsibility. He married Martha Parsonage and they had ten children of whom the seventh, James, was to be my well-remembered grandfather.

Not content with just the turtle business, George and his brother, James, my great great uncle, had set up the Reversionary Property Company, buying, leasing and selling property, mainly in Liverpool, and a very successful enterprise it turned out to be. One story relates that a stationery shop in Castle Street, Liverpool, had been bought for £45,000 in a morning and then was sold for £52,000 that afternoon! Who remembers the prestigious Waring and Gillow shop in Bold Street? when that business was first set up, the premises were leased from the Reversionary Property Company. That family link will be referred to later in my story.

With the family's businesses' success George (senior) was able to move to Egremont, on the East Wirral coast. In 1867, George purchased two fine houses North Meade in Brighton Street, where Wallasey (now Wirral) Town Hall replaces it, and Hope House in Victoria Road (now renamed Borough Road), Seacombe. The Hulses were 'carriage folk' and had living-in servants. According to records, the family lived in the houses or let them out, until 1898, when both were sold. George had died in 1871, leaving trustees to manage the properties. My great grandfather George had continued to live at North Meade and it was there in 1881 that my dear grandfather James Edwin Hulse was born. His own career began by joining the family property business until his marriage to Margaret (Maggie) Pickering on 24 April, 1905, at St Bede's Church, Toxteth. Maggie's family's farm at Pulford, near Chester, was close to the Duke of Westminster's Estate. James and Maggie ran a dairy business in Edge Lane, Liverpool, before changing to managing a series of licensed premises, mostly in Liverpool, including, I was told, the Crown in Lime Street at the junction with Skelhorne Street, and the Cattle Market Inn at 329, Prescot Road.

When the First World War was declared in 1914, James, at the age of 34, enlisted on 4 September; he was posted to the 2nd Dragoon Guards, his regimental number being 9869. While still in training he had an accident; I was told that he had fallen off his horse. As a result, he was discharged on sickness grounds on 15 July, 1915. He had not served long enough to bc cntitled to a pension, however, he was awarded a Silver War Badge (No. 70340) to show that he had enlisted to serve his country, but had been unable to continue his training because of sickness. I suppose that, in one way, it was fortunate that he had not been posted abroad; anyway, he was able to return to being a licensee, the last premises that James and Maggie ran being the Birkenhead Arms, which was later demolished to provide a wider entrance to the Birkenhead Tunnel on the Wirral side of the Mersey. In due course they moved to Prestatyn where they ran the Sunset Hotel; I shall tell you much more about that in my own story.

My father, Robert Edwin Hulse, was born in Seacombe in 1906, the eldest of five children. He served his apprenticeship as an electrical engineer, working for the appropriate department at Waring and Gillow's premises in Bold Street. In his spare time he played rugby, football and cricket; a keen runner, he joined the Liverpool Harriers and what is more, the Eastham Harriers! When he was 21, his grandfather George Hulse (junior) died, on 29 September 1927. George had retired firstly to Spring Bank in Mollington, then had moved to Oakfield Grange in Great Saughall, not far away. A widower, George had married his housekeeper, Annie Ellen Blackman, in 1921. In spite of his age and his damaged arm, he had played a full part in local activities, including horticulture and bowls; in addition, for several years, he had been a member of the Mollington Parish Council.

Have you ever been involved in the matter of a family Will? sometimes, there are many unforeseen complications, as I now realise. George (junior) had become a wealthy man and, with foresight, he had appointed trustees to manage his estate; sure enough, an initial distribution took place but, remember, George and Martha had had 10 children, so even a large amount of money would have had to be divided up between them and any other beneficiaries, including his widow and step-daughter. Even so, we of the succeeding generations are still awaiting the final 'winding up' of the estate. A large metal box, full of legal documents, with their convoluted wording still exists, but one shudders to think what solicitors would charge to establish the final resolution...

Life went on; my father with his electrical skills soon found ready employment, especially as there was a surge in house-building between the wars. Government subsidies were available both for council estates and for privately-funded properties; of course, all had to be built to certain standards and, by then, electricity was to be used, although street lamps were still normally gas-lit. In addition, older dwellings which had always relied on gas lamps or even just candles and oil lamps, were generally being adapted for electricity.

The family's hard work and entrepreneurship qualities led my father, Robert, and his brother, William, to take over Roberts' old premises at Bromborough Cross where they sold bicycles and batteries and it became a base for their electrical business.

In about 1934, having sold the Birkenhead Arms, and having part of the family inheritance, my grandparents, James and Maggie, were able to purchase one of the new semi-detached houses on the Woodlands Estate on Bromborough Village Road. They lived there for a short while before moving to Windle Hill Farm near Willaston, before their final move to Prestatyn.

Beau Décor - (behing Muffs the Butchers in Bromborough)
This was the first home of my Great Grandmother Rosena Roberts, bringing
up five children here. It was originally part of the stables of Kettlewells Farm.
Robert, my Great Grandfather was a coach driver and a horse trainer.
In those days, before the A41, the coaches travelled from Birkenhead through
Bromborough, Eastham Village and on to Chester.

White Row Cottages where my Great Grandmother Rosina Roberts moved to
from the Beau Décor who was Bromborough's first midwife
- (opposite the surgery in Bromborough)
These cottages were opposite the now Doctors surgery in Bromborough
Village. Mrs Pink Eye lived in one, I was told she was the first person
to cultivate the pink eye potato.

*Mother (Ursula) front row, second left on an outing
with school friends in the 1920s.*

*Alfred my Grandfather in his first car, bought from Sir William Forwood,
Bromborough Hall. He used the car for his first taxi service in
Bromborough in 1921.*

Roberts Garage first premises at Bromborough Cross.
Grandfather Alf had the first hand turning petrol pump.
In the 1920s they sold cycles, paraffin and had a taxi service.

Roberts Garage when first built on the A41 (New Chester Road)
before Christ the King Catholic Church was built.

Garage Advert.

*Plymyard House – rear view circa 1900. Situated on Bridle Road and
New Chester Road. This was a country mansion, owned by the Ravenscroft
family where my mother and her brothers played music for their house parties
in the 1930s. It was used as a surgery during the war.
Today Treetops Surgery has replaced it.*

Eastham Ferry Hotel and gardens.

This photo shows the Hotel in all its glory with the Jubilee Arch celebrating Queen Victoria and the beautiful wooden verandas enclosing the Hotel. They were removed by builders when renovating in the 1960s to a public outcry.

Entrance to Eastham Gardens and Hotel.   Nr. Birkenhead.

24

*Mother on beach
at Prestatyn, 1936.*

*The Dolly dancers.
Ursula, 2nd right at the Lido Prestatyn, 1940s*

Opening of Roberts Garage on the New Chester Road with all the staff and family: Mother Ursula, Father Robert, Uncle Claude, Aunty Olga, on front row; in the middle Grandfather Alf and Grandmother Emma; second row; in the middle, Uncle Ken fifth from left.

Chapter Two

Bromborough Beginnings

I was told that I was born on 11 January 1937 in the house next to the Garage while a snowstorm raged outside! I grew up in a very busy place. Mother and Uncle Ken were in the office, Father was occupied with his electrical business and, at first, Grandad Alf and Nan Emma were always in the background. Naturally, I do not remember the smallpox and diphtheria inoculations received at the Council Offices in Allport Lane, nor do I remember the declaration of War on September 3, 1939, but there are many, many things which I do remember. As my mother was so busy, Olive Byrom, who helped in the office, also cared for me part of the time; I liked her very much. In addition I had a very good nanny – Mrs Wheeler who lived at Carlett Lodge, where the St John Ambulance building now stands, close to the New Chester Road.

Schooldays! My first school, and really my favourite one: Mrs Pattison's Bromborough Preparatory School situated in a lovely old Victorian house named The Allports, just by the Common, only a short distance from home. I loved the walk through the Common and into the grounds by a little side gate, an easy distance for a four year old, as I started school in 1941. Two years later, my brother Bobby joined me. Near the school, and opposite the Methodist Church in Allport Lane was a big dark disused quarry; of course we were not allowed near it. For a while we lived in Woodyear Road, just a little further to walk.

The school uniform in winter, for girls, comprised a bottle green coat and hat with a gymslip of the same colour, together with a cream blouse; in summertime I wore a blazer, panama hat and green check cotton frock. The school grounds were so attractive: the lawn was circled by trccs and I recall especially a large willow tree. I always looked forward to Dollies' Day, which was the last day of school, before the summer holidays, when we were allowed to take our dolls' prams to school and were treated to a tea party on the lawn, under the willow. This tea would consist of small cucumber sandwiches, jelly and fairy cakes, and it is a memory I will always cherish.

My English teacher's name was Miss Allen, who was tall and slim with dark, curly hair and a lovely smile. She was a ray of sunshine in my life and I learned so much from her; the way she taught was wonderful, kind, funny and serious by turns. Many times she would give me a note to take home to my mother, inviting me to her home to tea on a Sunday afternoon (I was always reminded not to tell the other children!). I remember her mother's lovely iced lemon cake and the swing in her garden; I would swing high into the sky, having a great time, without a care in the world. The highlight of school was a story at the end of the day, read by the wonderful Miss Allen.

There was a pupil in my class who was so naughty and who seemed so often to be sitting in the corner writing lines – 'I must concentrate'. However, and very pleasingly, when we met again, a few years ago, I heard about a very successful career, running an IT business.

I must mention my brother, Bobby, again; he was two years younger than me and a real 'tinker'! At first, he did not like school, so my task was to take him there in the morning and to make sure that he stayed there as, on a few occasions, after assembly in the hall, he managed to slip away! One day he vanished and I was called on to help look for him; Mrs Pattison had telephoned my mother at the Garage, informing her that Bobby was not at school. My mother and Grandad Roberts came at once in the old Daimler car and picked me up. Off we went, down Allport Lane and then turned into Acre Lane. There were fields on the left hand side, before the houses were built, and we spotted a school cap bobbing up and down in the growing crop; the grown-ups gave chase, caught Bobby and took us both back to school. Of course, after a while, Bobby grew out of his truancy and settled down. I shall tell you more about Bobby in another chapter.

What else do I remember about those absorbing, happy and quiet seven years at Bromborough Preparatory School? the lessons, of course, which included the usual English, French, Sums, History, Geography, Music (including piano lessons) and P.E., the latter in Mrs Weaver-Smith's classes. Mrs Pattison was most particular about good manners, thus reinforcing what we all learned at home. I owe a great deal to my first school for the fine, all-round education, and for getting to know the fellow-pupils, among whom I particularly recall Sheelagh, Alison, Graham and Marjorie Thompson, Jeremy Kettle, Philip Bastow, Margaret Jolliffe, Diane Griffin.

During the War, one item which each of us had to take to school was the little cardboard box, slung over the shoulder, containing the all-important gas mask; thankfully, they were never needed, but the mention of them brings me to my next chapter.

Advertisement published in Gore's Liverpool Directory

*George Hulse senior
Turtle Merchant, Property
Developer, Exotic Animals
Importer, bringing the first animals
into the UK that started Zoos.*

*Great Uncle James – A Naturalist
in the family Turtle business and the
Reversionary Property Business.*

Ann Hulse.
Great Great Grandmother Mother to ten children, living at
Hope House, Wallasey, in later years.

Hope House, in Liscard Wallasey in the 1800s with great grandmother,
uncle John and a young niece.

Grandmother's wedding at St. Beads Church, Toxteth on 24th April 1905.
Maggie Pickering, a farmers daughter from Chester married
James Hulse in 1905.

My Grandparents with my Father, baby Robert.

My great great grandparents, the Pickerings Farmers from Pulford,
Chester circa 1800s.

My great grandfather George Hulse junior at his estate in Mollington,
Chester, who survived after his arm was badly mauled by one of the lions
he had brought from Africa to sell to zoos across the UK.

*Great Uncle Richard Hulse
a Cotton Broker, who lived
in Wallasey.*

*My favourite Uncle Ken
who was in the 8th Army
with General Montgomery
one of the desert rats.*

Chapter Three

Ursula on the Home Front

In the dining room of the house next to Roberts Garage, stood the indoor shelter to protect us when the air raids were on; I remember vividly that I used it as a tap dancing platform!

When we lived in Woodyear Road, our Anderson Air Raid Shelter was at the far end of the back garden; we went down steps to get into it and it always smelt musty. 1941 was a bad year locally for the Blitz caused many deaths and a good deal of damage and destruction. I recall one particular time when my mother drove me down Green Lane (nowadays only for pedestrians) to watch Liverpool burning, such an eerie sight from across the river and clearly visible against the dark sky. Another night, my mother woke us up about 3 o'clock, telling us to get up immediately and go to the shelter; I hastily tried to fasten the buttons on my 'liberty bodice', then finished dressing and picked up the basket with milk and sandwiches, which were always prepared ready for just such an emergency, and we collected our gas masks, before hurrying down the garden path. My mother was so nervous, especially when a delayed-action bomb dropped nearby, blowing out many windows locally, and causing other damage. What made it much worse was that Father was in danger.

During the War, Father's electrical skills were very much to the fore; he worked for Martin Hearn at Hooton Park, a most important air field with all the associated workshops. He was the supervisor of 200 workers and Father had an additional responsibility, that of testing the electrics on the Mosquito aircraft while they were in flight. That particular night, the regular flight to Hatfield was undertaken; thankfully he returned safe and sound.

Blackout curtains were essential in every home, it was just part of life in those days. Identity cards were issued, and we all had ration books, which were registered at one of the local shops; Hodgsons, for example, at Bromborough Cross, or Mr Frank Neal's shop in Bromborough Village Road. How well I remember Mr Willie Hodgson with his large, old-fashioned, hearing aid.

Petrol was rationed, and not everyone had cars anyway. Of course the Garage was very busy, not only providing petrol, but also repairing vehicles, including farm ones, and running the all important taxi service. We employed nine staff, at that time and were open around the clock. In 1937, in response to a circular letter from the Council, Grandfather Alf had offered two taxis and one private car with four drivers, when required to assist in any forthcoming emergency situation.

A well-remembered poster was worded 'Dig for Victory' and showed a spade being dug into the ground. Many, many local people, already used to productive gardening, set to, growing chiefly vegetables and fruit, often enough rearing hens and rabbits as both eggs and meat were on the ration. Pig swill was collected as local farmers and even other people reared pigs too. Allotments really came into their own, for example the ones next to the Bradmoor and those wartime ones on Mendell grounds, bordering Allport Lane, where the school now stands, and others where Christ the King Primary School is now.

Nan and Grandad Roberts assiduously cultivated the land to the rear of the Garage, the apples and the carrots, onions and other vegetables were carefully wrapped in brown paper and stored in racks in the shed. Nan busily bottled soft fruit and made jam.

In 1941, an extra sugar allowance was announced, as the fruit crop was so good. Before fridges were widely used, we had a meat safe to keep flies away from the food, and a marble slab in the larder was a cool place for the milk, blancmange and junket. Sometimes Nan and Grandad had help in the garden from a few soldiers based at Carlett Park, a very short distance away. The Army was stationed there in what was known officially as No.76 Transit Camp, housed in specially built huts for the men, while the Officers lived in Carlett Park House itself, originally home to the Torr family but, more recently, a Noviciate for the Christian Brothers, a Catholic Teaching Congregation. I remember the camouflaged army vehicles positioned under the trees: tanks, bren-gun carriers and lorries. I recall the German planes flying along the river, seeking their targets which included oil installations, factories, docks and railway stations. Eastham Locks were also under threat.

The soldiers' huts, up to 80 in number, built of brick and concrete, housed about 2,000 men over the years, and as it was a transit camp, there was constant movement in and out. In 1946 the Army finally left Carlett Park and the huts were then used as temporary accommodation for people made homeless during the War. I recall visiting one of our Garage staff who lived there; Gwen Bakewell was on call. With her son, Gwen had made their home as cosy and welcoming as possible, with seats on both sides of the hut, and the beds at the back. A wood burning stove was in the centre, its chimney went up through the roof.

Eventually the huts were vacated and, in 1952, the College of Further Education was established at Carlett Park; some of the huts were then used for about 10 years when the last remaining ones were demolished.

Uncle Ken had joined the Army during the War and was in the North Africa Campaign. One leave, he arrived at Bromborough Preparatory School to take Bobby and me home – the other children were greatly impressed, not only by his very smart Captain's uniform, but also by his splendid red M.G. (T.C.)!

Around that time, Grandad Roberts decided to retire, well, he still kept a very keen interest in the Garage, so it was not really a retirement. Nan of course found that their new home – a cottage next to Knockaloe, an old Victorian house on Bridle Road, offered even more scope for gardening activities as the kitchen garden for the big house contained not only apple, pear and cherry trees, but also fruit bushes and vegetable plots. While they lived there, I walked the short distance from school to have lunch with them; everything was fresh and beautifully cooked, another very happy memory.

Another cherished recollection of Nan Roberts was learning from her how to bake bread and churn butter – both using traditional methods; the result was truly delicious. Another treat was being allowed to look at her button box; it was square, made of raffia and had a handle at the top. All shapes and sizes of buttons filled it right up and I was allowed to tip them out and arrange them according to colour. As we sat by the roaring fire on a winter's evening, I was taught how to crochet, knit and embroider, skills for which I am truly grateful.

Council Offices in Bromborough – mother and her brothers played here for dancing on Saturday nights. The Co-Operative is now built on this site.

Bromborough Preparatory School situated on the Common, Allport Road.
This was my first school from the age of 4 to 11 years. I loved it here.

41

*This is my school - Bromborough Proparity School
on the common on Allport Road.*

*Ursula and Bobby in the
garden at Woodyear Road, my
little doll Suzie is on my knee.*

*Grandad Roberts
in the Garage garden.*

Granny Emma and mother in the Garage garden – in between being bombed.

Mother, Bobby and I in the Garage garden.

Chapter Four

Welsh Interludes

As I mentioned earlier in my story, Grandfather and Grandmother Hulse had moved to the Sunset Hotel in Prestatyn. There is such a lot I recall of that place as, during the War, and even after it, I was sent there to stay in school holidays. Bobby, being younger, stayed at home, and the invaluable Mrs Wheeler helped to look after him. Little Ursula was put on a train at Chester General Station, carrying her small brown suitcase. In those days the Guard would be requested to keep an eye on such important passengers! The journey was lovely; I used to sit by the window on the right hand side of the compartment so I could enjoy the beautiful views – first, of the River Dee, and then the open sea – all fresh and sparkly.

At Prestatyn Station I was always met by one of the maids from the Hotel; she would carry my case for the short distance to Sunset. The Victorian reception area had a turkey-red carpet, large brass gong to summon guests to meals, and large grandfather clock that sounded out the hour with a lovely, lilting, mellow tone.

I would be taken up to Room Four on the first floor; I called it The Blue Room because of the lovely décor on the curtains, bedding and the pretty print cushion on a sweet little chair. There was a wash stand in the room (before en suites), this was a piece of furniture which had a marble top with a tiled splash-back-and-sides border, a cupboard underneath contained spare towels. A large bowl, soap dish and matching water jug (filled and brought in by the maid) occupied the top. The towels in use were laid out on a dome-shaped stand close by. Each bedroom had these as there was only one bathroom on each floor. Under the bed was placed a glazed earthenware chamber pot, some had a floral

Grandmother Maggie and James Hulse.

decoration. Downstairs we kept the two warming pans, provided to warm the guests' beds. They consisted of a copper container with a long wooden handle and red-hot ashes were placed into the pan, the lid carefully secured and the warmer was then slipped between the sheets - a very effective way of preparing the beds on a cold night. Additionally, 'stone' hot water bottles were in use.

Grandfather James was not physically fit enough to manage the day-to-day running of the Sunset, so Grandmother Maggie was in charge. The clientele catered for were usually holiday-makers but, during the War, there were quite a few Canadian pilots and their wives staying there while the men were waiting to be posted to the various squadrons. Sunset was always full, a bustling place – there was never a dull moment.

Grandmother, of course, had the office duties to attend to as well and, in the evenings, would be working on the accounts. Her private lounge was very cosy - she had the most comfortable, feather-filled, large settee that one could sink into on sitting down. Grandmother said that it had been very expensive when purchased at Waring and Gillow in Bold Street – then a very prestigious area. The family there were friendly with my grandfather James and, of course, my own father had served his apprenticeship there. In later years I too was able to buy my own feather-filled three-piece suite at Waring and Gillow!

An accomplished needlewoman, Grandmother taught me, when I was old enough, how to use the treadle sewing machine; when I was 15, I was making my own dresses, thanks to her tuition. The lounge also housed an H.M.V. wind-up gramophone which had a big, tulip-shaped speaker, and the large, old-fashioned records were played, once the needle had been placed on exactly the right place in the record itself. I was in my element as I always loved to sing and dance, so the opportunity for displaying these gifts was there.

On Sunday afternoons, Grandmother would invite Mr Bradbury-Jones, the local vicar and his wife, to a traditional afternoon tea, carefully timed so as to fit in between the Church Services. The usual fare offered consisted of sandwiches, made of brown bread and butter, complemented by home-made damson jam housed in a pretty china jam pot or on an attractive glass dish. After that dainty cakes, displayed on a 3 tier cake stand would be offered; the tea (leaf of course) served in delicate china cups and saucers. The well polished knives and spoons and the spotless napkins were taken for granted.

One such afternoon, Grandmother made her usual request – I was to recite some poetry, so I obliged. Grandmother clapped her hands and then announced that I was going to dance for the guests and wound up the gramophone. The record I had selected was a Charleston, called Black Bottom and I started to dance with gusto. As I got into the routine, our guests' faces suddenly turned to horror - I was too young to realise that such a dance was a 'no-no' on the Sabbath! I left the lounge in shame, with my head down, and was never asked to do a repeat performance.

Another occasion when I blotted my copy book also happened at a weekend when three of my Hulse cousins arrived to stay at Sunset. The cook prepared the usual 4 o'clock afternoon tea, and on the table was a simply beautiful cake with a magnificent meringue 'ball' on the top – so tempting. The cousins dared me to put my finger into the meringue… when grandmother found out, she was 'not amused'; immediately I was sent up to bed – ne tea, no supper, and no books! It was a very hard lesson.

Nevertheless, in other ways, I did make myself really useful at Sunset. There was always work to be done, of course. Younger folk nowadays would find the following details quite surprising.

The farmhouse-style kitchen housed a cast iron Victorian range, which had to be black-leaded; how well I remember the Zebo polish! Brasso was used for the bars. On the usual swing hobs stood the large black kettles with their constant supply of boiling water. The range was mostly used for bread baking, while two gas stoves were much in use for other cooking.

On one side of the kitchen was a large, roaring fire, pulley racks were to one side – more about that later. Often enough I was one of a chain of four at the sink for the washing up. Another of my duties was to put the silver away into a large sideboard, where the drawers were lined with the traditional green baize; everything had to be placed in the correct compartments:- knives, forks and spoons, noting the different sizes for the various uses. The pearl-handled fish knives and forks had their own special boxes, which were then carefully closed with a hasp. After meal-times, I would help the maids, using silver-backed brushes with the accompanying crumb trays, to brush the table cloths.

Also in the kitchen was the mop cupboard, containing such a variety of mops:- wet ones, dry ones, polishing ones and many more. There were at least two vacuum cleaners; at this time there were no fitted carpets. Everything was spick and span, including the brass stair-rods. The pantry housed a very long slab to keep things cool as the only fridge could not contain everything.

Another clear memory of helping out at Sunset was in the Hotel's washhouse. The laundry comprised, for example, bedding, towels, tablecloths, table napkins, tea towels and the maids' uniforms: black dresses, white caps and aprons. The laundry procedure was as follows:- first the rubbing board was used, where appropriate – it was a ridged metal board where any collars and cuffs and stained items would be scrubbed, using a stiff brush and hard soap. Next, the galvanized Dolly Tubs were employed for soaking the various items, as needs be overnight, in very hot water in which soda crystals had been dissolved; then the Dolly Peg came into its own: a long wooden pole with a bar attached part-way down. A disc near the bottom guarded three little 'legs' which pounded the washing as one grasped the hand-bar firmly, twisting it backwards and forwards. After that and when appropriate, some of the bedding would be put into the large gas boiler. Rinsing took place in the large Belfast sink with the last rinse containing 'Blue' for white materials, with starch when needed, being added later before the strenuous work with the mangle, ensuring that the items were folded correctly, a daunting task with pure linen. The ironing, which I was never allowed to do, took place on the well-scrubbed, kitchen table which was suitable covered with thick material for the task. The several flat irons, up to six as I recall, were heated by the fire and a thick oven-glove type of protection was worn to avoid burning one's hand.

Finally, the two long pulley-racks were loaded and hoisted aloft so that the airing could take place. On wet days, there were three big pulleys in the washhouse annexe, to help with the drying. How times have changed!

As a little aside, I would like to tell you about some of the living-in maids. They had their own dormitory accommodation in the grounds of the Hotel. Grandmother always chose to put the advertisement for the maids required in the Manchester Evening News, and she was particularly prepared to employ unmarried mothers, who came with their babies. I remember helping to look after the little ones, up to three at any one time. A while ago, one of these babies, now of course a grown woman, contacted me to thank me for helping to look after her.

Well, back to my main story; there was a radio in the Hotel, and I remember a very special occasion; I must have been eight years old at the time. Once again, I had been banished upstairs for some misdemeanor, but there was such a noise in the reception area that I could not resist peeping through the banisters to see what was going on. The guests were crowded around the radio, shouting for joy. Grandmother saw me, and to my great relief, she called out 'Come down darling' and she hugged me. The War was over (V.E. Day 8 May 1945), everyone was in a good mood and I will never forget the look of relief on their faces at that moment.

Mother and I on the beach at Prestatyn.

Southport Bandstand outside the hairdressers shop where I worked in Lord Street, Southport in the 1950s. On summer days I would sit listening to the band whilst eating my lunch.

Oakdene Filling Station, Ulnes Walton, Lancashire.
Old photo circa 1950s and today.

Dave Hickson when he was playing for Everton Football Club.

An illustration of an old pram.

Dave Hickson a year before he died.
Left to right: Tracy Austin, Barbara Carrington Stan Boardman the comedian,
Dave Hickson and I.

Chapter Five

New Beginnings

Peace meant that people could begin the slow recovery from all the difficulties experienced during the War. Of course, rationing for many items continued for nearly ten years and, although new houses were being built, all that took time.

My father, fortunately for him and his 20 employees, had plenty of work in the locality as he had won a contract to install electricity in the new properties, and even older ones, for example, Burleydam in Childer Thornton, which was still a family house. In addition, he set up a shop at the side of Roberts Garage on the New Chester Road in Bromborough, selling electrical goods and Raleigh bicycles and parts; he had a depot and a shop in Willaston Village too. The Hulse name was becoming really well-known.

Roberts Garage, itself, had escaped war damage and the work there continued, increasing over the years; it was very much a family concern. Uncle Claude supervised the five mechanics of whom, in due course, my brother Bobby was one. Uncle Ken, my mother and Olive Byrom continued their invaluable work in the office. Of course, in the family tradition, I was roped in after school, when I was old enough. I worked in the shop at the side of the garage; in addition, I cleaned out the oil cabinets, washed the petrol pumps down with paraffin, and scrubbed out the house – the ground floor had all stone floors so I worked very hard, but I loved it. Another task was washing and cleaning the wedding cars, which included Humber Hawk, Humber Snipe and a Daimler.

Taxis too were always in use; we had up to four at any one time, usually 'Bullnose' Morris Humber Hawks and an Austin 20. We ran a driving school with single manual control Morris Minors, by then driving tests were compulsory; when my mother first drove, there were no tests and she told me she had driven a Ford Unic in the 1920s.

Roberts Garage showing Christ the King Catholic Church circ 1950s. My Austin 7 bought for £11 is on the front along with one of our driving school Morris Minors.

The mention of school brings me back to my own school life, still, in 1945, at Bromborough Preparatory School. Some of my friends also went there, one I remember was Margaret Harding who lived in Allport Road, quite near the Garage; we played bat and ball in her garden. Among others from the school I recall were Pippa Eden, Sally Jones and Joan Dorricot, all nice friendly girls. Of course, there were my own cousins, Gill, Lydia, Colin, Steven and Malcolm, although I was more like a big sister to them. One special friend, who lived nearby, was Dorothy Lloyd (now Mrs Bartley); her father, Mr Charlie Lloyd, opened his own grocery shop at No. 900 New Chester Road in 1947 after having been Manager at Irwin's shop at Bromborough Cross. I remember especially one Christmas Day when Dorothy and I had each been given a doll's pram as a present; mine was a refurbished one and I was so pleased to have it, in those days, toys and dolls were greatly treasured as they were not plentiful. My doll was called Susie. How delighted we were to be able to set off for Torr Park in Eastham, unaccompanied, very proudly pushing our prams until we reached the lovely swings, where we seated ourselves, carefully holding our dolls and swinging gently backwards and forwards 'feeding' our small charges from a small 'baby bottle' which had a teat at each end. Eventually, we headed for home, rosy-cheeked and so happy to have had such a lovely time, just the two of us. Now Dorothy and I are both grandmothers, with years of experience in looking after real babies!

At Mrs Pattison's 'Prep' the time for the Common Entrance exam arrived, but I was so nervous and did not succeed in passing. Anyway, I went to Heygarth School and had begun to settle in. It so happened that a family move came under discussion, so my parents gave notice to the Headteacher that I would be leaving. However, the planned move was postponed as the place my parents had visited in North Wales turned out to be unsuitable. Oh, what about my schooling? The place at Heygarth Road had been taken, in expectation of my departure, so, the next school where I could be accommodated was Woodslee, not too far away so, off I went, and what a fortunate choice that turned out to be.

Miss Higley, the singing teacher told me that I had a lovely voice. I was in the school choir and Miss Higley said that I was to tell my mother to get my voice trained. However, mother was not interested; perhaps she felt that I should have a more academic career in mind! Anyway, later on, with money that I earned by doing chores at the garage, I was able to pay for singing lessons with Mrs Cheetam, a retired music teacher, who lived in Little Sutton in a large house with 6 cats which I remember very well! Mrs Cheetam taught me how to breathe from my diaphragm, when singing; the lessons continued for about 6 months. How grateful I am to her for her invaluable tuition which has stood me in very good stead, ever since then.

Inside and outside pictures of Shenas Coffee Bar – this was a successfully run business for 20 years.

*Leo Rutherford and Shena at the Odd Spot, Bold Street, a jazz club and casino
where we were resident for a year.*

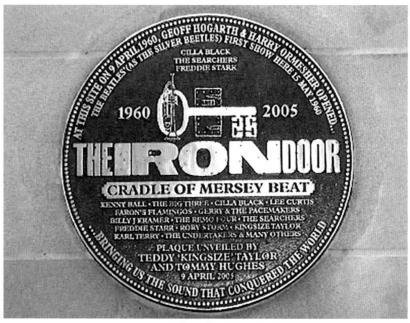

*Iron Door.
I sang here in the 1960s many times with the Ian Rutherford Jazz Band.*

An advert for the club command performance at St Georges Hall in Liverpool. I sang with the the Crescents and received a large silver cup, a fantastic night, 1959.

Alan Williams, the Beatles first manager, owned the Jacaranda Coffee Club in Slater Street, Liverpool in the 1950s and 60s. After my gigs at weekends, my nurse friend Barbara Carrington was always in the basement of the Jacaranda dancing with other nurses from Clatterbridge Hospital. I used to meet up with the Beatles in their coffee bar. The Royal Caribbean Steel Band played rock and roll, they were fantastic!

Beatles Statues.
These were outside my coffee shop Lucy in the Sky in Cavern Walks.

Lucy in the Sky Coffee Bar in Cavern Walks.

Alan Williams, the Beatles first manager, with me at the 2014 Beatles Convention at the Adelphi Hotel, Liverpool.

The reception at my Wedding at Eastham Ferry Hotel in 1960s.

Brenda and Bobby's wedding, 1960s.

Druid Inn, Llanferres, North Wales. We ran this pub for five years.

Bobby with some of the many trophies he won racing circa 1960s.

Bobby racing at Oulton Park.

Jason Hulse, Bobby's second son in action on a scramble bike.

Ursula singing at Mold Golf Club, North Wales, 2001.

Ursula singing with the Welsh Jazz Men at Abersoch Sailing Club, 2014.

My brother Bobby and Brenda's wedding, held at the Eastham Ferry Hotel.
Ursula and Robert Hulse, grooms parents, brides mother Nellie Kerr. Bridesmaids Ursula, bride's sister Linda, family members my cousins Gill Roberts and Malcolm Roberts, Aunty Olga, Uncle Claude, my lovely Uncle Ken, Kenny Kerr, the brides brother, Aunty Lila, Robin Simister a motorcycle entrepreneur.

Chapter Six

A Lancashire Life

It must have been in about 1950 when my parents found more suitable premises: Oakdene Filling Station, Ulnes Walton, near Chorley, and within reach of Southport, so off we went. We lived in the large red-brick house, where the front room served as a shop. On the road side was the petrol station and the café was located in a wooden chalet style building which had a large lawn leading up to it. As well as attending school (more about that later),I worked in the shop and café and on the petrol pumps, not only in the evenings, but also at weekends. In addition, my task after school on Wednesdays was housework; I took out the 'coconut' mat from the living room. This was made of parachute cord, with a wide mesh and so all the dust went through it, so I hauled it off to the washing line and gave it a real beating with the carpet beater. Next, I brushed up the dust (about a bucket full) I used, perhaps, three buckets of water and some bar soap and a scrubbing brush, to scrub the whole floor on my hands and knees, before putting the large mat back in place. All this was done in between eating tea, going in and out the shop and café and serving petrol until 11 o'clock at night. It was a hectic life and I often felt very miserable at that time.

It was hard not being able to visit Nan and Grandad Roberts, except on rare occasions, and my mother very much missed being at home in Bromborough. However, both my father and Bobby settled in better than we did.

Fortunately some really nice things happened, which I shall tell you about now. Soon after we had moved to Ulnes Walton, I became friendly with the Wharf family. Mr and Mrs Wharf ran the Rose and Crown Public House, opposite our Garage and with their three children: Joyce, Eric and Alan were friendly and welcoming. It was in the entertainment room, upstairs at the Rose and Crown, that I was able to sing to an audience, not just the family or in the school choir, but I shall tell you more about that presently.

Of course, I went to the local secondary school; it was very different from the ones I had attended at home in Bromborough and Eastham, and I never really settled in at all, but I do have at least two special memories which did help me. Every week, we had to write an English composition, and every week the English teacher asked me to read out mine as an example to the class of how to write well.

The art lessons were also times when I could do really good work; when I was 14, my painting of the Madonna and Child was entered in a Children's Competitive Art Exhibition which was being shown around the country, starting at the Harris Art Gallery in Preston. As a result, I won a scholarship to Southport Art College; what a lovely surprise!

I joined a sewing class in the Village Hall and classes for ballroom, tap and square dancing – something I loved. I must have got it from my mother who danced the Charleston, and it was my mother who took me to the classes and then home afterwards, so I was carefully chaperoned!

Well, it was just about that time that my singing was noticed more widely; the Rose and Crown had an upstairs entertainment room, with a stage. Like many teenagers, I was really into the new era of pop music coming on the radio – Alma Cogan, Petula Clark etc. and I had found an old gramophone on a rubbish tip; it had no handle so I would use my finger to turn the turntable, so that I could learn the songs on the records my Wharf friends lent me.

One evening, when I was in the entertainment room at the Rose and Crown, a band was rehearsing; it was the Fred Dickinson Band, and I was singing along with them because they were playing all the songs I knew. Fred said, in his lovely Lancashire accent, 'You seem to know all these songs, can you sing?' I replied that I thought I could and so he invited me on to the stage so that he could hear me. I sang Alma Cogan's Dreamboat and after my 'audition', Fred asked if I would join him and the group every Friday and Saturday.

This was going on at the same time that I was beginning at the Art College and already had a Saturday job – what a busy time! I was really spreading my wings.

Of course, I had to ask my mother about the entertainment opportunities; fortunately, she agreed, as long as I was safe going to and from the venues. Fred's wife would accompany me and the band was playing at such places as the Palm Court, Wigan, which was a very posh dance hall. It had a stage shaped like a pink open oyster shell which was very attractive. All the dancers wore evening dress and the band played foxtrots, waltzes, tangoes, cha cha and a little bit of jive. Another regular venue was Wigan Baths – they had a dance floor over the pool in winter. Preston and Leyland Public Halls were other regular bookings. I seem to remember earning 5/- for an evening; what would be the equivalent around today? £10? Or more?

The Saturday job? Just before leaving school, I had been fortunate enough to secure a post at a top fashion shop in Preston, called Nottingham House. Miss Moon (her professional name) was the owner and an ex model; she was tall, slim and very chic. Her husband was a small man and looked a bit like Alfred Hitchcock. I often wondered what the attraction was! Her business partner was her sister-in-law, Mrs Horrocks, who was married to a gentleman who ran cotton mills in Bolton, supplying fabric to Horrocks Fashion House that was very popular in the 50s. I loved the Horrockses dresses and I used to put away so much a week off my wages until I had paid for them.

Nottingham House was opposite Preston Town Hall, a very impressive corner building on three floors. The ground floor sold accessories, gloves, hats etc., the second floor was a showroom where all the Dior styles, Horrockses dresses and wedding gowns were. The workroom was at the top of the building.

My job, as a junior, included picking up pins, hand-delivering dresses, packed in large brown boxes, by bus or on foot, to the affluent people of Preston.

The staff were brilliant: Betty, the window-dresser, who was attractive and looked like Elizabeth Taylor, always dressed in striking colours - reds and blues. She was dating a Preston North End footballer and was one of the first WAGS.

Josie, who was in fashion sales, was a petite blonde and she was also going out with a professional footballer.

Julie, my friend, worked on the accessory counter. She was a very angelic looking, tall and a strawberry blonde who looked like Olivia Newton John. I can visualise her now, with her long hair, wearing a white blouse, black pencil skirt and black pumps - she was such a nice friend.

Julie and I would sometimes lunch at a little café next to the shop where I remember enjoying the most delicious mushroom soup with toast. At home, I was not allowed to wash my hair unless my mother agreed, so I would go to Julie's house and she would wash it for me.

I loved fashion and wanted to be a fashion designer. Some Saturday lunch times, I would sit in the workroom at the top of the building. All the alterations were done there and Ruth, the top seamstress, taught me the finer skills of dressmaking to add to the invaluable knowledge imparted by my grandmothers and the class I had attended at Ulnes Walton Village Hall.

My father was so strict; for my Saturday job, I could not wear clothes I had made, and had to hide them, so I would take a bag and change what I was wearing. He had bought me 'jack' boots from the Army and Navy and I think they were for men; I hated them. I had been given some lovely 'snakeskin' sling backs by a customer at our garage, a Captain's wife called Melissa; I used to babysit for her. Anyway, I would put the jack boots on and change into the sling backs. At work I would change into smart clothes other people had given me.

One Saturday, when I was returning home from work, I went to the hedge where I had hidden the jack boots and they were gone! I walked up to the big house to ask if anyone had seen them and the gardener said his wife had found them and was wearing them. She would not give them back to me but I didn't mind because I hated them. Guess what? Father went out and bought me another pair!

I loved the Saturday job which continued whilst I was at Southport Art College; I shall tell you more about my studies there. Starting at a new place was rather daunting for me, not least getting to know the other students. The first year was based on nature drawing, landscapes, fashion, clay modelling, textile design, still life and how to print on material. I really liked the course, but I was very shy when the nude model appeared, so I would stay in the cloakroom for the whole lesson.

After one year we went to an art exhibition to Hereford. On the way there, I was sitting alone in the front seat of the coach as I did not have a friend at the College, because I was so shy and awkward. A mature student came from the back of the coach, sat next to me and tried to kiss me! I was not having that so I stood on the seat, took off my cuban heeled shoe and hit him with it. He went crazy; he got hold of my arms and pushed me out of the coach window. The glass broke and I was hanging half in and half out of the window. I cut my face, although it did not really hurt me, I was very upset, so much so that I decided to finish my course at the Art College there and then.

That seemed, at the time, to be a real set-back; for weeks I could not tell my mother why I had resigned, because it had really upset me. The next few months were spent working in the Petrol Station and in the shop and café although I really disliked it; there was too much to do and my parents did not seem to appreciate my situation.

I felt so frustrated that, one day, I took up the phone book, jotted down some addresses and wrote to three hairdressers enquiring if they needed an apprentice. Two interviews resulted and I accepted one in Lord Street, Southport, just next to the Prince of Wales Hotel. What a relief! My cloud had a silver lining and I loved my new job; I was apprentice to Eddie Hamer, who owned Eileen's Hairdressing. We had many top clients living in Southport, for example in a road called Rotten Row.

Eddie had worked in London's Mayfair, starting his career as an apprentice to Raymond (Mr Teezy Weezy was his famous TV name). Among the clients at the salon there were Alma Cogan, Petula Clark and Georgia Brown; he also styled Shirley Bassey's wigs.

Eddie had moved from London, taking his mother with him, to a nice bungalow in Churchtown, Southport, and set up his own business. Already the various 'stars' knew him, and so they continued to be his clients, when on their frequent visits to the Garrick Theatre, which was situated practically opposite the salon. While Eddie continued styling Shirley Bassey's wigs, I shampooed Petula Clark, Alma Cogan and Georgia Brown's hair, and that of many more famous stars before Eddie did the styling. What is more, we would be invited to the various shows at the theatre.

After the shows I would always go backstage; I remember one occasion when Alma Cogan showed me the dresses she wore. She designed them herself and they were truly amazing: one had a skirt which resembled a powder puff of pale pink tulle, encrusted with little diamante decorations and a fitted, strapless bodice. Alma had short black, curly hair. I loved her singing and her personality. Sadly she died aged 32 - what a loss - she had many a 'top ten' record.

Eddie himself put on shows at the Scala Theatre, and I would learn the score of each musical and all the different parts – that's my 'showbiz' side!

Lunch-times were lovely; it was so enjoyable to be out for a stroll in the fresh air, gazing at the sea – always so far out in Southport. Sometimes I took a packed lunch down to the beach or to the gardens in the centre of Lord Street, where I could sit and listen to the brass band playing. Yet another venue, summer and winter, was a little café in the Arcade, where a trio of ladies would play chamber music.

Another memory of my apprentice days were the hairdressing shows at Blackpool, Preston and London; I had lovely thick golden-blonde hair and the girls used to use me as a model.

Those were lovely days with happy memories. However, when I came home, there was always work to be done. After my tea, I was in the shop and serving petrol until about midnight. The shop stocked a wide range of goods and we even had our own recipe for ice-cream, which was noted as the best for miles around; on summer Sundays, my job was to serve cones and wafers.

More good memories of our stay in Lancashire were of visits from Barbara Carrington, a Bromborough friend; I did look forward to the weekends when we met her at Croston Station. We really enjoyed each other's company and sharing our common interest in the latest fashions. Barbara was then a student nurse, starting at Clatterbridge Hospital's Childrens 'Wendy' Ward. Hers was a vocation which she followed all her working life and she has remained a good friend ever since.

On my infrequent visits to Bromborough, at that time, I was expected to lend a hand at the Garage, so I shall digress here to relate a special story about the now late Dave Hickson, my uncle Ken's best friend, when he was a First Team player for Everton Football Club. I was 17 and had just passed my driving test when Uncle Ken asked me to take Dave to the Ground; other passengers on occasion were Charlie Layfield, the trainer, Cyril Lello, Brian Harris, Jimmy Harris (no relation), Jimmy O'Neill the goalie and Ted Buckle. When Harry Gill, a local Councillor and Everton supporter, was Mayor of Bebington, he wore his Mayoral Chain to show to the tunnel staff and no toll was levied! When we arrived, I was treated to a seat in the Press Box. On one occasion when we were leaving the ground there was, as usual, a sea of fans surrounding the car, I remember Dave shouting that he couldn't shut the door because the fans had hold of his leg, trying to rip his trousers off! We got away with Dave missing a shoe, a sock and his trouser leg was all ripped at the bottom, he was such a star they all wanted a piece of him.

Dave Hickson was like an uncle to me, he was also a great friend of my family's over the years. He had a fantastic career and is still the only footballer in history to have played professionally for Tranmere Rovers, Liverpool and Everton football clubs.

Dave became poorly in 2011 and for last two years of his life, I helped to nurse him, I was able to take him out, and later visited him in hospital, one of many friends who did so. I would like to thank Colin and Lydia Roberts (Dave's Godchildren) Stan Boardman, Pete, Tracy Austin, Sonia and Phil from the Nags Head pub in Willaston, Ian and his wife, Derek and Julie Mountfield and Billy Butler for the wonderful eulogy at Liverpool Cathedral at his funeral, Bill Kenwright and least of all Harry Ross Chaplain of Everton for helping to give Dave such a wonderful sendoff. Dave was always a kind and loyal person, a true gentleman, now in heaven with uncle Ken causing chaos I'm sure!

Sometimes our time in Lancashire was difficult for me, but other special memories were the occasions when I attended Church, especially on the day of my Confirmation. As it happened, the Bishop of Blackburn was not able to officiate on that day so, to my great delight, the Bishop of Chester came to take his place; it was so comforting for me, and I treasure that memory.

Chapter Seven

Back in Bromborough: 'Opportunity Knocks'

In 1956 I was 19 and my four-year apprenticeship had been completed. By then both Grandad and Nan Roberts had passed away; A share of Roberts Garage in Bromborough was left to my mother, Ursula Hulse (née Roberts), so we moved back to Bromborough. At first, we lived in a detached house on Bromborough Village Road, just by the corner of Cambridge Road and, once again, I helped my parents and uncles Claude and Ken at the Garage on the New Chester Road. In our driving school we used four Morris Minors, which also provided the taxi service; wedding cars were usually Humber Hawks. Reluctantly, I became a driving instructress and I remember very well some of the people whom I taught, including Mr John Brown of Ferry Road, Mrs Kerruish of Spital and Mrs Andrews of San Diego, but living in Allport Lane, Bromborough, at that time.

Even before I was born, and when I was growing up, the family was always on friendly terms with the clergy at Christ the King R. C. Church next door to us; in fact, when the Church was to be built, we gave a piece of our land to the Diocese to assist the project. First came Father Campbell, next Father Pownall, then Father Velarde followed by Father Evans, and we got to know them all very well.

In addition to my work at the Garage, I was a mobile hairdresser, cycling round in a very stately way, on my sit-up-and-beg bicycle! That reminded me of the tales of my mother 'braiding' the back wheels of such bicycles to prevent the ladies' long skirts from catching in the spokes. I still enjoy that work, although I now travel by car.

I still wanted a 'showbiz' career, although unlike today, there were not many places to get started. Not to be daunted, I found an agent in Duke Street, through an advertisement for a singer in a show at the Pavilion ('Pivvy') Theatre in Liverpool, called the Back Entry Kids. I climbed up so many flights of stairs to the office that I was out of breath when I arrived at the top. I knocked on the door and a booming voice shouted 'Come in'. Sidney was sitting in a commodious chair. He was a large man wearing a Homburg hat and big overcoat and smoking a fat cigar. When I told him I had come for the singing audition for the show, his reply was 'Let's see your legs!' I told him in a shocked voice that I was here for the singing part, not to dance, and I started for the door. He asked me to come back and let him hear my voice, so I sang Bless This House. He boomed 'We are not running a classical concert you know'. However, I went on to star in the show, singing the Shirley Bassey number Big Spender, wearing a dress in leopard skin printed material that I had made myself, and I brought the house down. As it happened, I did not go on to that agent's books.

Also, in that particular show, was an up-and-coming comedian called Ricky McCabe; his father ran a pub round the corner from the 'Pivvy'. Ricky later became a successful theatrical agent.

About that time I was still at the Garage, just singing while at my work, when one day a lady came in to pay for petrol; she said 'You have a lovely voice. Would you like to come with me to the Crosville Bus Club in Rock Ferry? My son has a band playing there.' She did take me and I sang Getting To Know You from the King and I. Well, I had a wonderful ovation and, as a result, her son asked would I like to go to The Merseyside Artists' Association in Sheil Road, Liverpool. On Sunday afternoons, booking secretaries from local working men's clubs held auditions for prospective entertainers. Representatives came from quite a wide area:- The National Union of Railwaymen, North End Buffs, Bootle Dockers, Walton Trades and Labour, Clockface Miners (St Helens) and Speke Labour for example. For my audition, I sang Ma, He's Making Eyes At Me; before the afternoon ended, I had

Saturday night bookings for the next few months.

I sang at the Bootle Dockers' Club. Two hundred Dockers and their wives were saying 'Go on, entertain us Queen!' I gave my music to the band. Alfred Rafe was the piano player - he had his hair parted in the middle, I recall. There was nearly a calamity as he couldn't read music and played wrong notes. I thought I would 'die a death' which in singing terms meant that I would not get a clap or get paid. Frantically I looked at the audience and in the middle of the front row, a little man was sitting. He had a bald head, I invited him 'Come on up and help me with this song'. I sang a comedy number called I Want a Man and it too, brought the house down. His wife shouted up to me 'You can have him, Queen!'

Thinking back, so many memories come readily to mind that, really, because I performed at some of the venues several times, it is not easy to put them in date order, and other, more domestic matters had to be juggled as well.

One special booking involved singing for the prisoners in Walton Jail; of course, security was paramount, as I soon discovered. A quick visit to the loo was somewhat prolonged by the discovery that I had been locked in, and the prison officers had to get me out, just before the second act. Johnny Kennedy was booked with me, as he was on many other occasions; he was a great singer and always very popular - I felt as though I was always in competition with him.

Every week I went to Mellor's newsagents, conveniently situated at No.896 New Chester Road, for my copies of The Stage, New Musical Express and The Mersey Beat, the latter edited by Bill Harry. As a follow-up, I went to London for a few auditions and, while there, I went into the coffee bars which were sprouting up in Soho – for example the 2IIs (Two Eyes) and the Freight Train run by Nancy Whiskey and Chas McDevitt, where I met Cliff Richard, Billy Fury and many others.

When I came home, my mother expressed interest in the coffee bar scene; I think it was really because my parents preferred me to be at home and, ideally, available to help out at the Garage. It was in 1958 that we embarked on opening Shena's Coffee Bar (my stage name was Shena) in premises at No. 914 on the New Chester Road, close to Roberts Garage at Nos. 892 & 894. It was very successful, not only with the local youth, but also with the students at Carlett Park College, very close by. The juke box, which we installed quite soon, was an added attraction. The passing trade made full use of our facilities, motorists, motorcyclists and cyclists all called in, finding a modern coffee bar was just what they wanted, including hot snacks and my special apple pie with cream or ice cream. In addition to Espresso, Cappuccino was available and we were amongst the first to have a Gaggia machine.

Of course, I was particularly interested in seeing the various band members – Billy Butler and Chris Wharten called in on many a Friday night; Billy's order was always 'Hot dog, no onions, no mustard.' He had the first disco in pubs in North Wales, and has gone on to be a popular stalwart on Radio Merseyside. I shall tell you about other famous names, later on. When I think back to the throbbing sound of the Mersey Beat music that filled the City air, the 1950s and 60s were the most exciting time I had ever encountered and the best of it was that I was right there at the beginning of a new musical era.

Relating to my cabaret engagements, which I slotted in with my hard work at the Coffee Bar and, occasionally, at the Garage, I shall try to include the ones which stand out.

I recall the first time I met the Leo Rutherford Jazzmen; it was a charity night at the Peel Hall in Liverpool. After I had sung, they asked me to join them; in the band were Leo on clarinet, Dave Dickson, Brian Hall on guitar, Aynsley Dunbar on drums (he later played for Fleetwood Mac) and, lastly, Richard Stilgoe on piano. Now, Richard was a maths and music teacher at Mostyn House School in Parkgate, West Wirral; he lived in an old funeral hearse in a car park in Liverpool, and was such a character – on one occasion he was dressed in a Rupert Bear suit and he wore a red, flashing, dickey bow. Another night, he got down on one knee and proposed to me – I replied 'Oh Richard, you are so funny, get up off your knees and get back into your hearse!'

He was such a talented musician; he went on to fame and stardom with TV shows and radio programmes, and writing hit musicals with Andrew Lloyd Webber and Elton John, one example being The Lion King. To 'cap it all' he has been Knighted.

What about the others? Dave Dickson now runs the Peninsula Jazz Band and Brian Hall went on to write the hit song Amanda – with Stuart Gilles singing it, the record was in the top ten for several weeks.

With Leo's Jazz Band, I sang many times, at the Iron Door, a warehouse basement club at No. 13 Temple Street. I parked my first mini, jumped out with my bag of music, and trip-trotted down the cobbled street in my stiletto heels. In the 1950s one could park, more or less, anywhere – no double yellow lines, no parking meters, no traffic wardens and, of course, not nearly as many cars as nowadays. It was great. After a gig, I used to drop off the boys in the band.

As well as being at the Odd Spot 89 Bold Street, other venues where we played included the Caldy 7s Rugby Club; Hoylake Sailing Club, West Kirby and at many a 21st birthday party around Wirral.

Fast forward a few years - Fort Perch Rock, New Brighton, was a really amazing place, and I played there with Leo's Band. My Ford Popular had been replaced, eventually, by a TR4 sports car in bright red. The place was packed, with people dancing to traditional jazz. We were completely unaware that the wind had got up and the resulting sea swell at high tide had covered our vehicles. Eventually, we realised that we were stranded until the elements were more favourable. Needless to say, the TR4's bodywork was ruined.

Now wind back the reel - I sang at the Compton Club in Mount Pleasant later to become the Mardi Gras, not far from the Adelphi Hotel. At that time it was run by a Mr Cook and his family. The daughter had a very lavish flat above the club complete with a pink poodle. I really appreciated the family's kindness towards me.

I did weekends there with the comedian/singer Johnny Hackett; he had a fantastic act. In addition, one night, he reluctantly auctioned his white sharkskin jacket that someone had brought him from America – it went for 10/- (50p), which was not bad in the 1950s, when money was really tight for many people. I am pleased to say that Johnny Hackett finally was able to set up his own club in Spain and it was a great success.

For a while, I was the resident at the Pink Parrot, a cabaret dance club in Duke Street. I sang there with the Del Tones, a great band, led by 'Frankie', and we played there a great number of times. In 1959 I was chosen to appear at the Merseyside Artists' Command Performance at St George's Hall, and the Del Tones backed me. It was a night to remember – I sang Blossom Time and got a standing ovation. Weeks later, at Ozzie Wade's club in Everton, I was presented with a large silver cup for my performance, the presentation being made by Tom McGee, the Honorary Secretary of the Mersey District Social Club Association – MDSCA.

Another venue for me was the Latin Quarter a basement club, off Dale Street, with a spiral staircase leading down into the club. It was owned by 'Sonny' Timpson and his girlfriend, Marge. They had the first local glass dance floor in different colours, very stylish, and they catered for high-class professionals. A trio named The Cassanovas played there; later they reformed as The Big Three, with Adrian Barber on guitar and Johnny Hutchinson on drums. Adrian had a flat in Faulkner Square, with his girlfriend, Terry. He had been a ships' electrician and he would build all the amplifiers for the groups of the time, in his flat, which was a mass of wires. Eventually, he went on to run the Peppermint Lounge in New York.

I had a real surprise on arriving at the Golden Guinea, at Egremont; I parked my Ford Popular in the road that still resembled a bomb site. My friend, Barbara said 'There's no club around here, it's all derelict'; but I knew that it was the correct address I had been given, so we walked along and, seeing a large door with a light in the middle, we realised that this must be it. Babs was adamant there was no club around but I knocked on the door anyway. When someone opened it I had the shock of my life: revealed was a wide staircase with a plush carpet leading up to the club area. There were chandeliers and glitter; I had never been in such a lavish nightclub! I was on with Paul Melba, an impressionist, and Eddie Flannigan, a comedian. The club owner was John Stanley, a local entrepreneur, who went on to own the Kraal Club in New Brighton. The Kraal held one night folk singing sessions; old bus seats were fitted in the upper area and the basement was where groups played – the Lettermen being a regular band.

New Brighton became a big club scene: - the Chelsea Reach, Late Extra, Penny Farthing and the aforementioned Kraal Club were popular in the 1960s and 70s with people flocking there for a night's entertainment. I sang at the Embassy Club in New Brighton's Victoria Street.

Now, another venue, a little further away, was an interesting one: Chirk Castle, where Alan Williams, through the Jacaranda (more of that club later), ran a barbeque in the summer. Lots of people went and cars were parked all around the castle grounds. A big bonfire was a memorable attraction and we sat on bales of hay, enjoying the Royal Caribbean Steel Band playing. I left at about 3 a.m. with my nurse friends, including Barbara; the problem was that they were on duty at 6 am and should have been back at the nurses' home at Elm House, Clatterbridge Hospital. Anyway, on such ventures, they would leave a window open, but if Matron discovered that, they were in trouble!

I must mention some of the other artists appearing at the clubs. One was a comedian named Georgie Thornton, so funny.

I was booked to appear with him at the end of the show; we did a double act and, once again, brought the house down. Georgie wore a Teddy Boy suit, made out of a sack-sized Tate & Lyle sugar bag and had a fake wig, with a ponytail, like the one Max Wall used. We ended the night with rock and roll songs – very popular. Georgie was Cy Tucker's uncle and we often went for TV auditions – also there would be Jimmy Tarbuck, for example. Some people succeeded, others did not. I did go to the BBC in London for Bid for Fame auditions, did one show, but got voted off on the second one! Other well-known names on the club circuit were comedians Sonny Jones and Eddie Flannigan, the ventriloquist Roy Minting, impressionist Paul Melba, and, but by no means least, Frankie Vaughan and Tom O'Connor.

Sometimes, the London auditions resulted in a tour; the first one I got was with Cliff Richard and The Shadows, appearing for a six-week run around the country including the Liverpool Empire Theatre for a week - it was great. Also on the bill were Des O'Connor, a young comedian, and the Most Brothers. Mickey Most went on to be a big record producer, Lulu being one of his recording artists.

One summer season of shows was with Tommy Cooper - he was hilarious and I thoroughly enjoyed it, though as I did not drink or smoke, I was not into socialising in that way; Tommy, however, lived life to the full.

I was learning a lot about showbiz, but when the tours ended, I would go home to work at the Coffee Bar until the next job came up. In addition, I helped out at the Garage; there I continued to teach driving and to help with our taxi business. One very important contract was with the Mersey Docks and Harbour Board (as it was then) to provide a taxi service for the Mersey River Pilots of whom there might be as many as 176. They did, and still do, irreplaceable work, involving unsocial hours, so we assisted where necessary in driving them to, for example, Point Lynas on Anglesey. On occasion, I was able to entertain my passengers by singing to them, while travelling. Yes, included among such passengers was Stuart Wood, now retired Senior Mersey River Pilot whose broadcasts on Radio Merseyside are so much enjoyed and appreciated.

As if all those family activities were not enough, we opened a bed and breakfast facility at The Woodlands, on the opposite corner of Woodyear Road from the Coffee Bar.

Back to the local club scene- here are some memories. In the true Morcambe and Wise tradition: all the right information, but not necessarily in the right order! Yes, I did appear with those two pre-eminent entertainers; it was in Paignton in Devon for a four week show which included June Crane; and yes, the duo were unforgettably funny, and such a pleasure to know.

Everton Supporters' Club was a great venue. I remember appearing there with Johnny Kennedy; I had learned the new Petula Clark song Sailor the afternoon before and, as usual, Johnny was fantastic.

In the 1960s, new clubs were opening up all over Liverpool. The Cabaret Club was in Duke Street and I was there the first week it opened - Albert Dunlop, the ex-Everton goalkeeper, was the compère and Frank Ifield topped the bill, he was very handsome and was top of the charts. As a cabaret club, the dining area was all around the stage, the glamorous ladies showing off Liverpool fashion at its best. This was sophistication, nothing like the North End Buffs in Bootle or the Dockers' clubs, NUR (National Union of Railwaymen) or Walton Trades and Labour! While on that subject, there was also the Wheeltappers and Shunters' Club where, as with all the others of that kind I have listed as examples, these were for down-to-earth, good, working class people who were out to have a good time - these were the audiences I loved best of all: 'Go on, Queen, give us another!' was the cry that would go up from these folk, the salt of the earth – no wonder I loved them. Perhaps, especially so since I had had a very strict upbringing with no sentimentality, and these were warm-hearted people, so ready to show appreciation. Ask any professional singer or performer about the 'buzz' they get from such an audience.

However, entertainment was not always sweetness and light. I had a bad experience in the early 1960s. At that time, I had joined a rock band called Bopping Billy, we did gigs mostly in Chester and North Wales. One particular gig was at the Downtown Club in Warrington and on the bill was Screaming Lord Sutch. He used to swing into the audience as though he were in the jungle, wearing a loin cloth and the girls would scream as he fell amongst them. Also performing one night were Freddie Starr and the Midnighters; at the half time interval, for a joke, the piano player locked me in the dressing room with Freddie - I was scared stiff, banging on the door shouting 'Let me out!' while Freddie was looking in the mirror admiring himself, asking 'Don't you think I'm lovely?' - I got out as quickly as possible, what a relief... At the end of the performance, the band and I had to weave our way through the girls, who were crazy for the boys, and off we went in a cramped Austin A40 van, with the axle nearly touching the road!

Chester was a favourite place for me. The Riverside Dance Hall, on the banks of the Dee, was a good venue; the large hall had a sprung dance floor. We rehearsed on a Wednesday night, and were joined by local dance couples who were practising for a TV show. Our performance was on a Saturday when the Peter Dee Orchestra was resident. I remember that we had a lot of American airmen from Sealand Camp near Queensferry, and they partnered the girls as the dance music played. They loved to jive and showed the local girls all the new steps on the dance floor!

The Peter Dee Band moved to the Locarno Ballroom on West Derby Road, Liverpool. This was the most lavish ballroom I had ever seen, and there was a beautiful stage and a sprung dance floor. It was jam packed with dancers and there was a great atmosphere.

Back to Chester - I was asked to perform at the Oaklands Hotel on Hoole Road. It was a 1930s style hotel, run by Dora and Gerry Heathcote, catering for tourists and various visiting politicians; the hotel had 30 bedrooms and a basement night club. What do you think? When I was asked to perform there, Mr Heathcote had a 'limo' sent to my home in Bromborough!

The trio I sang with, was very talented. Once I sang with Yana, a chart topper of the day. Sometimes, Johnny and I sang duets, to his piano accompaniment. One night, a gentleman came in and sat by the stage; word got round that it was Edward Heath, a politician. Later on in the evening, his aide came over and asked would I like Mr Heath to play the piano for me? Johnny stepped aside and Edward Heath played On the Street Where You Live to great applause, and he complimented me on my voice. He later became Prime Minister.

The Oaklands Club became so very popular that, at weekends, people would queue to get in. We had so many of the Chester society folk, including beauty queens and models, and I remember this as being a 'fab' time in my life.

It must have been in about 1959 when I met the Beatles. I had heard about them around town but, as I was in the club circuit, I had never played the Cavern, which had opened in early 1957. On the night in question, I had dropped off my nurse friends, one of whom was Barbara Carrington, and arranged to meet them at the Jacaranda in Slater Street, later that night, when I had finished my gig. As I walked into that club, I was confronted by four young men, all in black leather. John Lennon came forward and said 'Who do you think you are, Alma Cogan?' He was very abrupt; I replied that I was a singer from Wirral. 'Oh, Wirral', John said, 'they are all stuck up over there!' I said that 'they' were not and we got chatting. His bite was not as bad as his bark.

Just then, Barbara came up from the Jacaranda basement, very hot after dancing to the Royal Caribbean Steel Band playing Rock and Roll; she asked me 'Who are these scruffs you are talking to?' Ouch!!! The Beatles scruffs? She has been eating her words ever since…

I met the Beatles over a few Saturdays and felt that John had a chip on his shoulder, having lost his mother just when he was getting to know her; he seemed to me to be a little lost boy, at that time.

Each of the Beatles, to me, had his own charisma; Pete Best was so, so handsome; Paul was the businessman; John, the talented, genial joker, and George was the shy guy.

Alan Williams and his wife owned the Jacaranda, and he was the Beatles manager.   He approached me with a view to doing a North West tour with them, but Brian Epstein came on the scene a few weeks after that, and the rest is history.

Well, back to the Garage; one day, I was in the office, giving change, when in walked John Lennon to pay for petrol. He told me they were off to London to record My Bonnie and I replied 'That's great!' I knew that Brian Epstein had taken them on as their Manager, and that they were, hopefully, on their way to stardom. John happened to notice the papers I bought every week, The Mersey Beat, The New Musical Express and The Stage. He said 'Oh, I can take those down with me and read them on the way?' I protested, 'I've just paid 6/- (30p) for those!', 'Oh, go on' he said, 'you know we're broke, with no cash!!!' He persuaded me, so I let him have them. Then he spotted a tube of Tunes throat sweets, up on the shelf; as singers in the 1950s and 60s, the mike and amplifiers were not as effective as they are today, and we always seemed to have sore throats; Fishermen's Friend were the ones we mostly favoured.   Anyway, he asked for four tubes of Tunes, and I responded by asking him for another 7/- (35p), but he had such charm when he wanted to, so I had to give in and let him just take them. 'When we are famous, I will always remember you' he said. I told him to go on and get into the car for London and, that too, is history. But he did repay me the debt, years later, when I was running my Lucy in the Sky café.

About 20 years ago, ITV asked me to take part in a documentary on the Beatles in the Jacaranda. The film crew took me into the basement where my nurse friends used to dance the night away, to the music of the Royal Caribbean Steel Band.

Back now to the early 1960s – about this time, through an advertisement in The Stage magazine, a different opportunity presented itself to me. I went to a London audition for a part in Sheridan's School of Scandal, starring Margaret Rutherford and, thankfully, I was successful. We went on tour to places such as Nottingham, Edinburgh and Liverpool. Margaret, and her husband Stringer, were very nice people, and I visited them at their home; they had no children, and they considered adopting me! However, my mother arranged to meet them and politely declined the offer…

Chapter Eight

A New Life

In 1965, I met and married Cliff Wilde, a marine engineer from Liverpool. At first, we lived in a semi-detached bungalow at Hooton Green; we had two sons - Clifford (junior) and Johnathon. I retired from singing, after about 200 appearances, but continued to help run the Coffee Bar and the Woodlands Guest House on the A41 in Bromborough. So, life continued to be very full, especially as Cliff was often away, as at that time he was at sea as a Second Engineer with the Blue Star Shipping Line.

A really heavy blow was suffered by the family in 1979 when my dear brother, Bobby, died; he was only 40. As he was two years younger than me, I was always his big sister; I loved him so much, although he was sometimes, at first, a little tinker at school, he was rather frail as a child so my mother was very protective of him, and he was not as adventurous as I was; he really made up for that later on!

Bobby had served his apprenticeship as a motor and motorcycle mechanic at the Garage, under the watchful eye of Uncle Claude. This stood him in very good stead, as he became, not only a skilled mechanic, but also a dauntless and successful trials bike rider and scrambler and a track rider, champion at, for example, Oulton Park, where he rode in side car events. In addition he took part in the prestigious TT races on the Isle of Man; all in all his many silver cups and other trophies remain a fitting tribute to his skills. Through racing, Bobby had got to know Mike Hailwood, a real star in the motor cycle world, having won major championships. In 1960, Mike's father, Stan, opened the branch of King's of Oxford motor cycle dealership, situated where Bromborough

Hall had once stood and where Matalan is today. After the dealership had been opened, I hosted a party at my Coffee Bar for everyone concerned.

Bobby married Brenda Kerr, and they had six children, my dearly loved nieces and nephews:- Wayne, Tracey, Tina, Emma, Jason and Lee.

When he died, it had such an effect on us all; in fact, my mother was devastated, and lived only for a short time after that. My parents had retired to a cottage in Eastham Village where they acted as a Bed and Breakfast 'overflow' from the Woodlands Guest House, taking in some visiting tourists, before my mother took ill. When that happened, I was so thankful to be near at hand, and able to nurse her at their home, for the short time she had to live. In 1983 she gently slipped away in my arms. I have the consolation of knowing that, after all, she said she was really proud of what I had achieved in my life.

In 1980 I had sold the Coffee Bar, followed by the sale of the Woodlands in 1984; also all connection with the Garage ceased. My next venture was the purchase of the Druid Inn, a country premises at Llanferres, near Mold, and I took my family up there, including my father and my brother's eldest son, Wayne. My husband was in Iraq as a maintenance engineer in the oil business, and so, when he returned, he, too, came to the pub. It had been run down, but I soon got it on its feet, with a disco, 100 seat restaurant, cabaret lounge and a top bar with open log fires; in addition we offered bed and breakfast accommodation and featured in the Welsh Tourist Guide at 5* rating.

To provide an added attraction, I contacted agents in Liverpool and had many acts on at the Druid Inn - and I always had a spot in the middle of the programme. We were so popular that people queued to get in. Among the bed and breakfast clients who came, we had actors and actresses from the nearby Theatr Clwyd, for example Vanessa Redgrave, Timothy Dalton and Seth Armstrong (the gamekeeper in Emmerdale Farm), and many other stage and TV celebrities.

After five years, we sold the premises and came back to Bromborough, eventually settling in a bungalow in Plymyard Avenue. Soon after that we bought the Bistro and Coffee Bar in Cavern Walks, Liverpool, later it was named Lucy in the Sky. I also used to sell Beatles' memorabilia and tell the tourists tales of the now legendary Four. The Japanese and Chinese tourists were always so fascinated and just wanted to hear a bit of history from someone who had been there in the heart of the Mersey Beat. By fortunate coincidence, a bronze statue of the Beatles stood outside my coffee shop, casting a shadow over it, it was quite a thrill to realise that. All this was when the shops were busy, and we did a roaring trade. The mother of Herbert the hairdresser had a little boutique in The Walks; she was a lovely lady and I still have many dresses I bought from her. Upstairs, was a Laura Ashley shop, some hairdressers, jewellers and a men's boutique.

In the late 1980s, I sold Lucy in the Sky as my marriage had ended; this was a dreadfully sad time for me, because I had been married for 23 years. However, things happen in life, so I dusted myself down and started again. My beautiful bungalow had to be sold, as I could not afford to live there anymore. At the time, I was nursing my father and I had one of my sons, and my nephew Wayne, living with me, too. It was so difficult - how I coped, I do not know, but I have a deep faith and believe these things are sent, and one gets strength from somewhere, somehow. Caring for my family has had a great impact on my life – I have learnt so much from my wonderful Roberts family and my grandmother Maggie Hulse, with whom I spent so much time as a youngster.

In 1992, just before the bungalow was sold, my father died, in my arms. I had nursed him for five years, and although he had always been very strict with me, I respected him always. Not long before he died, my father told me that he really admired the way I had conducted my life and how much he cherished the way I was looking after him.

A few weeks before he died, I took him to Eastham Woods, in the wheelchair, and we ended up at the Ferry Hotel. He always had a Bells' whisky and a sandwich and we sat outside in the late autumn sunshine, watching the tankers go up river to the QE2 oil dock by the entrance to the Manchester Ship Canal.

While we were there, two gentlemen came into the hotel and said 'Hello' to my father who told me 'That is Sam Couch, one of the Mersey River Pilots.' As I have mentioned already, we had driven many of these men in the 1970s and 80s in our taxi business at the Garage. The two men brought their pints and sat outside on the veranda with us. The other man with Sam felt he knew me from somewhere and my father later told me that he was Peter Baines, a Manchester Ship Canal Pilot. They took the ships up the Canal, the Mersey River Pilots having brought the ships from the Bar at the entrance of the Mersey, up to Eastham where the Manchester Pilots took over the vessels.

When I got chatting to Peter, it turned out that he had called at our Garage at one time, when his friend's motorcycle that he was riding, had broken down when he was on his way to sit the exam for his Master's Ticket, and Grandad Roberts arranged to have it mended for him at Bob Simister's premises in Rock Ferry. I had been in the office when Peter collected the bike and he remembered me, but I could not recall his visit.

Sometime later, Peter told me that he had worked on the canal for 28 years, and was living in Llandegla, North Wales. He had been divorced two years previously, and had his son living with him. I said I was also divorced, but, privately, I was wary of getting involved again, so soon.

Peter told me he was going on holiday to Florida, with his son, and would call me when he returned. He contacted me for weeks until I accepted his invitation to go to a bonfire party at the Crown, in Llandegla. I went reluctantly, but ended up having a lovely evening. His house was in the village, and we went back there for supper and I met young Pete. Our friendship had started; it was simply a 'brother and sister' relationship, all the way through. Pete had the same old fashioned principles that I had. He was kind, funny, loving and caring, and he treated me, almost the first time in my life, like a lady; Pete always remained a gentleman, he was a real 'elder brother' to me.

He was still a Canal Pilot and he had been trained as a Naval Cadet on the Conway, an old, wooden, battle-line ship, the third and last of that name, and first used as a training vessel in the Mersey in 1876, but transferred to the Menai Straits in 1941. It remained there until 1953 when loss of the vessel meant a shore-base for all the trainees. Pete said that, when he was there, it was a Spartan existence – rats were plentiful, but the food was not, so friends sent food parcels. At that time the cadet officers were linked with Gordonstoun near Inverness, Scotland, so after two years on the mother ship (as Conway was called) then they had a year at Gordonstoun. Several of the Royal family were educated there.

Pete remarked that, compared to the austerity of Conway, Gordonstoun was like Heaven, even having to get up at 5 am, take a freezing cold shower, then a five mile run, he loved it!

In 2009, we went to Gordonstoun and he showed me all over the grounds, and the dormitory he was in, and the main room with the Royal portraits on display. It was a wonderful day. Before that, we had been to Glasgow, to a Conway Club Annual Dinner Dance - we attended one every year at different venues.

In the years I was friends with Pete, we shared a little cottage at Abersoch on the Llyn Peninsula, a wonderful spot – coastal walks in the day, and a log fire in the evening. In addition, we travelled to America, Canada (including Prince Edward Island), Australia, Majorca, Italy (including Pompeii), Ibiza, and many other places. Pete loved to revisit places he had been to when he was a Captain with the Union Castle Line, sailing from Southampton. He also went regularly to South Africa and loved Cape Town.

Pete recalled one particularly memorable voyage in the 1950s, when his Union Castle ship was under contract to the M.O.D., conveying a special cargo to the Suez Canal. On 9 July 2006, he was one of a number of men receiving special medals from the Queen at Buckingham Palace. It was a most memorable occasion. Following that we went to a 1940s themed performance at Horseguards Parade where we were seated next to the Chelsea Pensioners and Yeomen of the Guard and not far from the Royal Box. It was such a hot day, but we thoroughly enjoyed the spectacle of Vera Lynn, dressed as a WAAF, driving a wartime jeep; in addition Bruce Forsyth was the compère, suitably dressed for the occasion, and Bradley Walsh and Joe Pascal sang Flanagan and Allan songs. Afterwards we all went up the Mall to witness the wonderful spectacle of the Red Arrows, followed by the Battle of Britain Memorial Flight. By this time, of course, the members of the Royal family were on the Palace balcony.

Finally, we went to St James's Park, where a Victorian-style tea party provided a welcome rest in the shade.

All this happened against the backdrop of the 7/7 London Bombings, two days before so there were many armed forces personnel in evidence with tanks placed close by.

Pete sadly passed away in 2011.

Now, here I am, in 2014, with so many memories – but what am I doing now? For the last five years I have been one of the 'Wirral Witches' (Women in touch with Claire House) a support group raising funds for Claire House Children's Hospice at Clatterbridge. In addition, I am on call as a film extra, working on Coronation Street, Emmerdale, Hollyoaks, and for advertisement filming. However, at heart, I am still the stage struck little girl who tap danced on top of an indoor air raid shelter in the Garage parlour whilst Ursula (senior) played the piano.

As I look back on my life so far, yes it has had many challenges, but I wouldn't have changed it. My elder son Clifford, in the family tradition, has his own garage business; married to Sandra (née Worswick) they have two lovely children, Callam and Lucy. Jonathon too has his own business and he and his wife Gill (née Tsang) also have two lovely children, Nathan and Sadie. All of them are my inspiration.

And Bobby and Brenda's children? All six of them are doing very well – the three girls are in the nursing profession while each of the three boys runs his own business. Bobby would have been so proud of them.

Croft Car Sales owned by Cliffe Wilde son of Ursula on the Croft Business Park in Bromborough. Following in the family tradition.

Chapter 9

Eastham, My Beautiful Village

Today I live a couple of miles down from Roberts Garage on the A41. I have lived in Eastham Village for 13 years now. When I was a little girl, I used to stay with aunty Olga and uncle Claude, who lived in the village then, behind the Stanley pub (now the Montgomery restaurant).

I have fond memories of Eastham Village. I remember playing with my cousin Gill when we used to play in her grandmother's little cottage that had a secret garden with a playhouse where we spent many happy hours; from here we could also watch the cows coming out of Masons farm. There was the popular Lancasters Bakery next to the Stanley, it was run by father and son and the smell of freshly baked bread wafted all over the village.

Another childhood memory is of the little shop at the lodge, which was by the park on Eastham Ferry Road, run by my friend Arnie Ward's mum; we loved buying gob stoppers! Arnie Ward and his family were lifetime friends, he was such a lovely man; also John Brown, who I gave driving lessons to, when we had the driving school at Roberts Garage, I remember him asking what to do when he approach traffic lights, I replied "put your foot down!" John often recalls this incident; we always laugh, what was I thinking of? Other friends include David Allan who along with John now run Eastham Archives keeping detailed information about the life and times of the village including a fantastic photographic history, they also organized an excellent WW1 exhibition at St Mary's Church with our wonderful vicar Beth.

As a family we would visit the Eastham Ferry Hotel regularly, I remember a scary incident there when I was 10; the family were having tea in the lovely gardens, there were two large goldfish ponds with lilies all over them. I was looking into the pond when I saw a knee surface, I moved it with my hand, it was my cousin Henry drowning! The family rushed over and dragged him out, he was taken into the kitchens where they pumped his stomach, I remember seeing tadpoles coming out, but he finally started to breathe. I had saved his life! The owner of the hotel, Aubrey Hewitson was so relieved he gave drinks all round.

The Hotel was family run, Aubrey's brother and sister in law worked there as well as his mother, who was the cook, I also remember Mrs Mac who was the manageress; they were always very busy even through the war, with captains wives staying there whilst waiting for the ships to come in. They had the main hotel accommodation for years and in the 20s mother and father enjoyed dancing the night away in the ballroom at the rear of the hotel, my mother said they were wonderful times.

Eastham Ferry Hotel was very busy in those days, with the boats coming and going, bringing people from Liverpool, the bluebell woods were a big attraction, also there were live bears in a bear pit, it still stands there today in Eastham Woods, however, there are only wooden bears now!

My wedding reception was held at Eastham Ferry Hotel as was my brother Bobby's when he married Brenda. I still visit the hotel and enjoy walking in the beautiful woods that I have known since childhood. I am pleased to say that my children and grandchildren have always enjoyed the wonders of Eastham Ferry too.

Eastham village as it is today. What a beautiful place to live.

With Celebrity Friends

An early picture of me singing with a rock band at the Downtown Club in Warrington.

Me appearing with the Duo Tones at the Druid Inn, Llanferres.

Ursula accompanying Mike Baldwin of 'Coronation Street' fame opening a newsagents in Bromborough. Ann and Phill (standing on my right) now own the Village News in Eastham Village.

Ursula and
3 Degrees Sheila Ferguson at
a Claire House function at the
Hilton Hotel 2014.

Ursula with
Elsie Tanner.
Coronation Street.

Ursula and Shirley Morrison at a Charity night for Claire House at Eaton Hall, Duke of Westminster's home, 2010.

Ursula and Sandra Williams at a 40s Charity Night in Heswall Hall in 2014.

With Family

Lucy Wilde my beautiful grandaughter studying medicine at Liverpool University and Barbara Carrington my lifetime friend who has dedicated her life to nursing, starting at Clatterbridge Hospital as a Wendy Ward Nurse going on to be Theatre Sister in Jersey Channel Islands.
A frequent visitor to the Jacaranda dancing the night away in Liverpool. The night I met the Beatles, Barbara popped her head up from the basement and said "who is this scruff you're talking to" it so happened to be that I was chatting with John Lennon, over the years I've said to her "what was he Barbara!"

Ursula with Peter sailing in Abersoch.

Acknowledgements

Thank you to my family, Alfred and Emma Lydia Roberts, my wonderful grandparents on my mother's side, James and Margaret Hulse on my father's side, for the wonderful love and devotion they gave to me all my life. My mother and father Ursula and Robert Hulse, the strict upbringing gave me courage and stamina to get through the obstacles I came up against on my journey through life.

Thank you so much to Susan Nicholson from Bromborough History Society for all the invaluable help, patience and kindness putting the book together, also Brian Nicholson, a great motorcycle enthusiast, for his great help with research.

Thank you to Cathy and Peter Grant, Literally Bookshop, New Brighton, for guiding me on the title of my book.

Also, warm thanks to Maxine, Allan and Ellie from Love Wirral Magazine, couldn't have done it without you, you are all fantastic.

Miss Allen, my English teacher from Pattison's Preparatory School, who had such a lovely smile and was so inspirational will always be remembered. Eddie Hamer, my wonderful hairdressing boss in Southport, best time of my life.

Barbara Carrington, a lifetime friend, she tried to keep me on the straight and narrow and failed for all the fun and laughter over the years. She dedicated her life to nursing, I admire her tremendously. Pete's river pilot friends, thank you for your friendship.

Ann Anderson, Bromborough History Society, who I sat with after school in the house in Bromborough Rake listening to her historical knowledge about Bromborough. Meeting Leo Rutherfored Jazz Band, great time in my life, Richard Stilgoe and I dueting, he was a true piano player. Brian Hall who wrote Amanda, Dave Dickson who now fronts the Peninsula Jazz Men, thanks for being a part of my life.

Special thanks to Margaret Rutherford, actress, who asked my mother if she could adopt me, my mother said, "certainly not!"

And lastly, to my dear and generous friend Alex Stewart. I must thank you for your encouragement in putting my memoirs down on paper! A true and loyal friend who I will always cherish, along with his wonderful children Graham and Alison and their families.

With thanks to:

Diane Heaton, Eastham Village resident for 32 years,
Karen Lundrum, Eastham Village Newsagents
Ann and Phil, Eastham Village Newsagents
Lydia and Colin Stevens, my cousins
Gill and Malcolm, my Roberts cousins
Ann Smethurst, my Hulse second cousin
Henry Hulse, my first cousin
Derek Hulse, my first cousin
Anita Hulse, my first cousin
Ian Boumphrey for help with photographs
Steph and Alison at the Photoshop in Bromborough Village

About the Author

Ursula Wilde was a singer in the 1950s and 60s at the start of the Merseybeat era in Liverpool. She became a business woman owning a country inn in Llanferess in North Wales, coffee bars including Lucy in the Sky in Cavern Walks in Liverpool, and also running a family with two sons Jonathan and Clifford.

She has always written in local magazines, History being her main subject, but this is the first autobiography publication on her life and times.

Ursula with her cousin Anne Smithurst ne Hulse tracing the family tree history.

Left to right. Callam Wilde my grandson, Cliff Wilde my son, daughter-in-law Sandra Wilde. Front row, Lucy Wilde my grandaughter and Cole Masters a friend of Lucy.